How Much Does It Weigh?

Contents

Katie Sharp

Rigby

We weigh things to tell
how heavy they are.
A feather weighs a little,
and an elephant weighs a lot.

How heavy are you?

Do you know how much you weigh?

How can you find out how much something weighs?
You can weigh it on a scale.
How many kinds of scales do you see here?

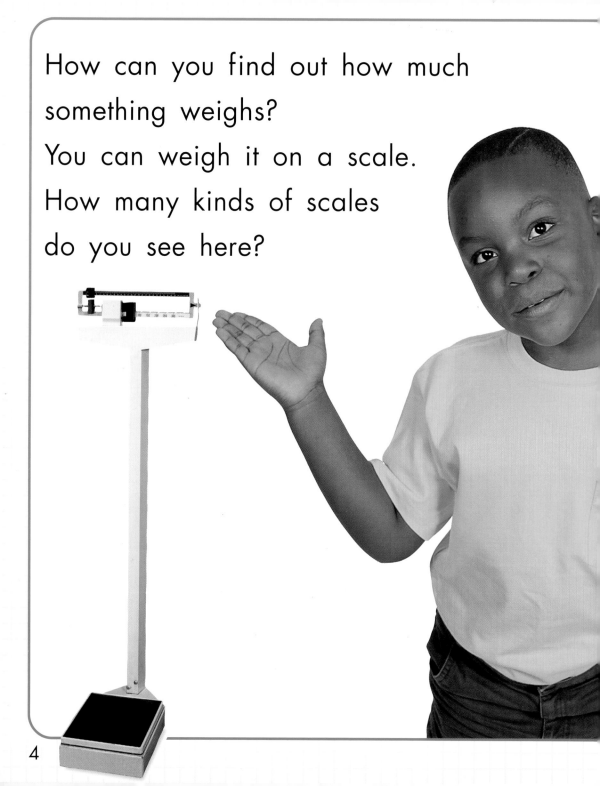

Kim and Henri have a scale at school.
The scale holds two pans,
and there's a long arm
between the pans.
Kim and Henri use the scale
to weigh things.

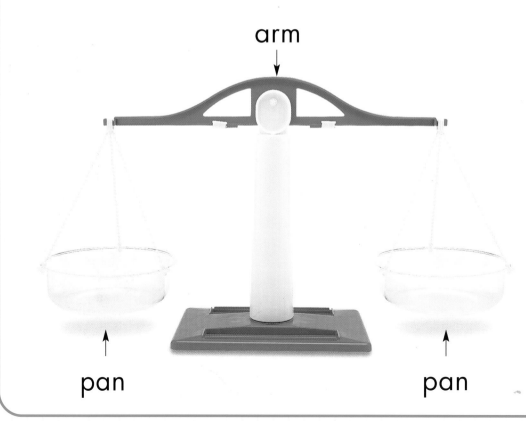

arm

pan

pan

Kim and Henri want to weigh a pencil.
Henri places the pencil in one pan.
Do you think the pencil will be heavy?
Let's see.

The pan that is holding the pencil moves down, and the other pan moves up.

Now we will see how much
the pencil weighs.
Help Henri and Kim find out.

Kim places a bear in the other pan.
That pan moves down, too.
The pans are now equal.
The pencil and the bear weigh
the same.

Now Henri and Kim want to weigh
a toy car.

Kim places bears in the other pan.

Help Kim count the bears.

1, 2, 3, 4, 5, 6, 7, 8, 9!

The pans are equal.

The car and nine bears

weigh the same!

Henri finds a book he wants to weigh.

He places the book on one pan,

and Kim counts the bears,

putting them into the other pan.

1, 2, 3, 4, 5, 6,

7, 8, 9, 10, 11, 12!

That's a lot of bears!